SMALL MATTERS MEAN THE WORLD

EARLY PRAISE FOR

# *Small Matters Mean the World*

❖

Often David Memmott's poems course like a "river of wind" to take us to where the world of the everyday meets the startling world of the strange with all its dangers. Allying himself with natural forces and animal spirits, he fashions a bridge between these two worlds to achieve a hard-won communion. A sturdy, detailed observer, and a faithful guide to the reader, Memmott becomes, in his own words, "a sound bowl of pure gold rung by thunder."

—JOHN MORRISON, author of *Monkey Island*

❖

In *Small Matters Mean the World*, David Memmott takes us on a journey through the liminal spaces in our lives—the space between the natural world and the human, the ephemeral and the familiar. "The evergreens lean to whisper/ in your ear. Lines that hold you together/ in a taut web..." Memmott creates that web with the tautness of his vision, holding us in it. His lyricism carries us on "A river of wind... toward the light," as the precision of his language reminds us, "The ancient/ world lies all around us with lessons/ to be relearned." But his greatest gift is that of the true seer, the one willing to summon those spaces, "Come finch, come flicker, come sundown,/ I track your workmanship over a high wire" and ultimately take the journey for us, "I stand alone, bent to the scent of your blood/ in black tracks on a field of white fire." In the end, this treasure of a book reminds us the answer to the secrets of the world around us have always been within.

—PETER GRANDBOIS, author of *Last Night I Aged a Hundred Years*

❖

David Memmott wants his readers to understand just how large the world is, and largely mysterious, even scary, perhaps even a shade crazy. This is why he uses such small things like the particularities of his backyard and neighborhood to illustrate his point. These poems about the comings and goings of birds and neighbors are some of my favorites in the collection. But as unwitting prophet, in other poems Memmott describes the sense of a wider world surreally encroaching suggesting it may be about to end whether under a hinted at dreamlike metaphysical threat or something as mundanely real as weather, man-generated wildfires, migrating birds or even the glimpse of a penitent traveler lugging a heavy wooden cross down the highway. The particularity of these poems keep us grounded and tethered and perhaps even comforted that Memmott is there to keep us informed and warn us about the true state of things under the surface of everyday life.

—DAVID MEHLER, editor of *Triggerfish Critical Review*
and author of *Roadworthy*

redbat books
pacific northwest writers series

# Small Matters Mean the World

POEMS

# DAVID MEMMOTT

redbat
books

redbat books
La Grande, Oregon
2022

Printed in the United States of America

First Edition: November 2022

Trade Paperback ISBN:  978-1-946970-08-4

Library of Congress Control Number: 2022947309

*Published by*
redbat books
La Grande, OR 97850
www.redbatbooks.com

Text set in Eidetic Neo OT

*Cover art by*
David Memmott

*Cover Design and Book Layout by*
redbat design | www.redbatdesign.com

# Table of Contents

*In a dark time, the eye begins to see...*
—THEODORE ROETHKE

# *Where the Bow Breaks the Wave*

Science tells us why we dream
even how we dream
but what we dream
and what it means depends
on endings concealed
in beginnings

The Mayans once reclaimed sacred ground
layering one temple over another
they remade their gods with scars
to reveal a hidden beauty

At the thin low line
where heaven touches the earth
a river of wind carries me
toward a fading light

I cannot hear my own breathing
cannot separate *inner* from *outer*
as my body drifts in primordial air
unbound from bubbles in melting ice

Where the bow breaks the wave
I dream in resistance
riding the bow wave
awake in the wake
of another landfall

that rolls me toward home

# I.

## Small Matters Mean the World

# Chasing the Dream

Between fall fires and after rain
the yellow hills of the Blue Mountains
come full shade at midnight.

From flash to flame, the goldfinch leaps
branch to branch at daybreak
captured in the still frame of my camera.

He returns to this crook in the apple tree
to build a nest only a stone's throw
from the sunflower patch.

Even with prosthetics for eyes
ready to zoom and focus, my binocular
vision cannot catch up.

He jumps from one energy level
to another like an electron
calling me out from within the lilac

from within the dogwood

from the other side of now.

## Wild Thoughts
### While Mowing the Lawn

Untended drought-dry edges
of our corner lot defeat the dream: earthly gardens
sculpted by human design into paradise
contagions carried overland to redeem
native ground with untended consequences.
In gestation I lie down on a summer night

roll onto my back kicking at a womb
freshly-mowed grass free of weeds, holding ground
with irrigation and fertilizer against morning glory,
a dim red tide of spotted spurge that squats
immovable between deck and garden.
I should respond with native force.

Redeem the garden by cutting loose native growth
to overrun false fences and rockjack corners
holding up lines against thickening yarrow, eruptions of wheatgrass,
crowns of wild rebellion that choke
the four-stroke engine that grooms the lordly lawn.

Beat back dandelions and thistle
unearthed across light years
by bringing back the soft dash
of lupine and camas and Indian paintbrush,
making room again for mullein and salsify
edible bulbs of blue camas and biscuit root
in grow boxes, mule's ears and bee plants
in raised beds, milkweed and dogwood flowering
out of cold volcanic ash.

Then invite the birds and the bees.

# *The Stump*

of the seventy-year-old
quaking aspen trips me up
every time I forget
how close I cut it
to the ground

unfinished business
blast it out
burn it down
pull it up with a John Deere
like a bad molar

no matter what I do
I'm laid up another winter
a boil on the butt of a bear
a stiff knuckle in my muscle
a sharp pain in the neck

I no longer see the face
of my stump as I buried him
but he hibernates there
in a hollow I never see
until I stumble

## The Answer

He announces himself with a drum roll.
I look up from my spade, leaning
into a ten-beat rest.
Call and response.
Is he listening?
Red-cheeked, black-bibbed flicker
peeks shyly around the telephone pole
where he bores the dry wood
like a cold drill.

I rap the shovel blade several times hard
against the fencepost
striking steel on steel
talking back.
Within seconds his answer comes
cracking the morning calm with a ringing retort:

*The sky is falling.*

*The sky is falling.*

# *Waiting for the Storm to Pass*

A strong cell tracks our way
out of the south. The first shout
echoes down the dun canyons as I finish
chores—mowing lawn, cutting broccoli, picking snow peas
the laundry *almost* drip-dry—when
thunder breaks and down pours.
Wind thins the pears barely holding the branch
as drops sharp as razor blades
split their skins.

The neighbor behind us lies on her death bed.
Her family gathers to clean out the house
tossing a lifetime of accumulation into the dumpster
untold stories stripped of sentiment and weighed for value
pulled from drawers
filling boxes for Goodwill.

My lawnmower chokes on the wet grass.
I ask her daughter if the end has come.
*Oh, no*, she says, shaking her head,
*she's still in there.*

# Harbingers

Starlings come down in a whiteout
a ravenous mob of hit-and-run marauders
rubbed out of nothing like a fearful frottage

The starlings come down to drive the flicker
from the nest like dive-bombers and raid
the unhatched eggs of beleaguered birds
cradled in the glistening webs of winter trees

They come down in a whiteout
with bickering beaks, disinvited to the dance
like the wild bunch shooting holes
in the dancefloor

They come down in a whiteout
wings iced with salve to stanch the wounds
of living too long in negative space

Out of nothingness they spin
like dead diatom shells settling to the bottom
of an internal sea in the deep where I drown

in the hold of a sunken ship
my bloated body rises, pulled
onto an ice floe by a black
horde of bickering birds

# *To the Squirrel Who Ate the Suet*

1.

You rascal, that sunflower seed
was never meant for you. I put out
those fat cakes in hanging baskets
to give winter birds a boost.
I kept vigil, marked their flights
in and out of the bare pear tree—owl-hawk
flicker, downy woodpecker—riding out the blizzard
aboard a peanut butter boat.

Not long after the junco arrive
fickle finch loosen and scatter the seed
and you jump in awakening the feral cat.
I went to add a new brick
and caught your act, hanging by hind
legs to steal the last
of the winter feed.

2.

When the birds have flown, the bottom
feeders show up making off with what is left.
You had me fooled for a while.
I blamed the starlings for hitting
the suet too hard. The trail
of peanut butter in shallow snow
incriminated you all the way to the telephone pole
your escape route to a swinging concourse
that carries you from neighbor to neighbor.
Where, I wonder, did you plant the walnuts
this year? I will know come spring.

Come finch, come flicker, come sundown
Who can blame you for doing Mother's work?
I track your workmanship over the high wire
watch your balancing act climax in a spiral
down to the ground like a pole dancer, quick
like a rabbit through the fence, broom tail
sweeping the snow in a flurry.

# *Winter Solstice*

This morning
I stagger out striking icicles
from my ears.

This winter depresses us all
Blue Mountains kicked back
under a frontal assault puts down a foot

in sweeping drifts. Oregon Junco
huddle like little monks in black cowls
palpitating under the Mugo pine.

Shagged elkhounds in ice pavilions
bay at the full moon and a kettle
drum plays in the wind.

I would have found my way back
into hibernation dreaming of lion
fish in translucent lagoons

a whale in the pale
waning moon
uncommon in any landmark.

A white world unmarked by trails
accretes by the inch overnight.
Cottonwood stripped of last leaves

knits an otherworldly calm
into the dense groan weight.
The lean years were half this harsh.

# *Why I'm Building a Privacy Fence*

In the window of my neighbor's house a red light
blinks red recording every movement I make.
One day the man behind the camera
strolls up the sidewalk and over the fence
assures me he cannot see me where I sit
most days in the corner of the deck.
So who's not a spy? I ask myself.
We all keep our eyes open, don't we?

The neighbor in the house behind us
died and left her house to her son who moved
into town with three aggressive Australian shepherds
farm dogs taught to tree a squirrel and kill a cat
were confined now to a minimum lot.
They dash front and back without ever tiring.
The camera guy captured on tape
every escape of that mad bitch
chasing joggers and attacking the mailman.

Whenever I'm on my bench on the deck
those shepherds line up chewing the wire fence
leaping berserk at the sight of our once feral cat, BG.
She kept the property free of rodents for years
left dead voles on the porch for us to find in the morning.

So when she's gone for days I have a look around
find her black and white corpse
dragged and dropped like a stiff rug
at the backstep in the farm dogs' backyard.

I go to the front of the house and knock
but he can't hear me above loud
speakers pounding the same dull thud over and over.

*

I finally decide on trespass to fetch back
the poor girl's broken body, hoping
he doesn't let his dogs out
not knowing I'm there.

We buried her in the garden
marked the spot with a stone.

Then one day camera man strolls casually
up the sidewalk and points to the rabid dogs
gnawing on the fence, dancing can-can up and down.
He has it all on tape, he says—the brutal murder.
The old girl got caught in the backyard
when all three dogs suddenly appeared
seeing a fat squirrel in their territory. She was too
fed up for winter to make fair game
so lost a couple of steps to surprise.

Camera man shakes his head in sympathy:
*Don't imagine you wanna see it?*

# In Potentia: A Re-Vision

*In essence, there is no universe*
*present without imagination...*
                    —FRED ALAN WOLFE

\*

The yogini flexes
to fix old scores
composed for upper
registers that fall
outside the event horizon.

\*

It's best to first consider
your keyboard:
a seven-octave concerto on, say,
a five-octave instrument
makes a completely different sound.
Lost chords absent grace notes and nuance
may still be enough to break
the silence.

\*

A collared dove
inside ribs of spruce
during a chance snowstorm
throws a blue falsetto.
Some hear music,
some hear noise.

Some conflate the thump of their heart
with the thud of snowmelt from a slumping evergreen.

*

The unnerving night grows thick
with weak talk;
you're overwhelmed already
by sound without sense.
Your yogini leans into Kundalini fire
that flares on perishable skin
burns away enough flesh
to describe the ineffable.

*

You bend backward
all the way to the floor,
to lost chords, grace-notes
and nuances in another register.

# Boys in Berries

Two boys on mountain bikes ride up the sidewalk next to our garden fence. They stop and inspect the blackberries, ripening under a limp sky. I am hidden by shadows on the deck, lost in stippled light behind wooden lattice.

*Are you stealing my berries*, my disembodied voice catches them unaware. They look up as I dismount from my perch on the porch to move the sprinkler.

*No, sir*, they sing in unison, bodies stiffening, caught red-handed with stained fingers.

*Of course you are*, I say, picking up the hose and dragging the sprinkler around so the spray will reach a neglected corner under the front window.

They must have been eight, maybe nine. One, in a Road Warrior helmet, looks defiant. The other, face concealed under a Fast and Furious motif knows instantly there's no sense in denying the crime. He drops his head. *Sorry.*

I set the timer and turn on the water. *Tell you what*, I promise, glancing at the boy who feels some degree of guilt. *If the berries you take are inside the fence, then you'd be stealing from me. But if they're outside the fence, well, then they're fair game.*

These rules were as clear as I could make them. Fast and Furious relaxed, lifted his head and nodded in agreement. He asks, *Can you eat the red berries?*

*Well, that patch there is blackberries,* I answer, *You can't eat blackberries until they're black. Red blackberries are bitter and could make you sick in the stomach.*

Most of the berries outside the fence were still red. They'll have to come back another day. Just before they mount their bikes and continue up the sidewalk, I point to another berry patch, where the berries were already picked or withered on the vine.

*Now those are raspberries,* I say. *You eat them when they're red.*

## *The Ragdoll Revival*

Mercurial spring delivers one last blow
as the sap rises. A great white swale
swallows the valley. Sudden hailstones
hammer heads of apple dolls
off their black branches. I burrow
deeper and go back to sleep.

Later, Honey paws the frozen turf
presses her snout against a scent
that runs underground like a vole.
In a vigorous tug-o'-war
she pulls up a ragdoll whose limp
arms slap wet muzzle.

I can't say how many times she's reburied
that ragdoll but it keeps rising from the grave.
She shakes its spineless body with worry
and whine. That doll must wear some scent
from another time. The ancient
world lies all around us with lessons
to be relearned.

*Dig deeper, little sister*, I say.
Some relic without an alibi
may swoon under scrutiny.
Do not trust the rootless to lie down
easy; they break their necks
on cracked sepulchers. Some new likeness
pokes its head out and civilization
stands on yet another educated guess

\*

another occluded vein
drawn from proximate shards.
Obsessed with digging up the past
our job is never done.

Honey combs the back yard over
for the right spot to re-bury that ragdoll.
Some loose soil around the compost maybe
or there under the burn barrel.

# *Pestilence*

Out of darkness comes disorder
clarion call of dogs barking at a shadow
that squats silent in the middle
of the road. The Shepherds next door
incite the Husky across the street to howl.
The black Pit Bull and white Samoan join in
Mayday duets broadcast through billowing
slats of green cyclone fence, a rolling
wave of dire warning.

Our Havoc picks up the beat at the southwest
corner, sounding off by the purple lilac.
His sister Honey comes in on the chorus
in good voice. They bounce off each other
like live wires, hackles up, alert to his presence
stopped still just outside the spot of street light
as if to gauge the calamity he provokes.

Face veiled in darkness.
Flick of a lighter, soft ember glow
phlegmatic cough and imagined rancid breath.
I call the dogs in, thank them
for being on alert. Havoc takes his treat
at the door and mounts the stairs
to bed having done his duty. Honey
drops her shoulder to the kitchen
floor, rolls over, exposing her pink belly
to a warm hand.

# Small Matters Mean the World

Eventually
    the yellow delicious apple tree
    sheds its fruit
    its limbs shaken from crown
    to root by a cloudburst

Apples
    fall into tall grass
    like lost sandlot baseballs
    in foul territory

Ants
    come marching one by one
    to claim a cache of cider-soft yellows—
    lightning-split.

Orbic weavers
    dance over shimmers of pure light
    where overripe fruit
    liquifies in the sun.

A conspiracy
    of yellowjackets, thirsty as sin
    climb out of broken skin
    red-eyed and mad as hell.

# II.

## *Some Nights My* Nothing *Rises*

# Path of Least Resistance

We roll off the assembly line licensed,
inspected, and quality-tested.
Buffed up and sold to the highest bidder.
The latest model engineered to stay within
the speed limit taught to settle
for the hum of steady progress.

We pledge to forego the danger
of ecstatic loops and black-out tailspins.
Given enough horsepower to climb
small mountains. Sold on the premise
that once over the top, balanced on the precipice
we coast in neutral in deliberate descent
without brakes, all the way down
onto easy street.

So much has been invested in us—
by bankers, teachers, parents, priests—to secure
a place in line
zombied by muzak
passively pummeled into heart failure
our debt reduced in small measure
by the frequency and duration
of half-truths.
They remind us constantly
how a straight tongue starves to death.

# Some Nights My Nothing Rises

I wake in a ghosted room
on a cold night. My body caught
halfway in another dimension.
*Nothing* rises to the bait
sowing uneasy silence

moves into my basement
to plan a takeover once the house
falls asleep. I am sequestered
in the kitchen brewing another spoiled
batch of philosopher's stone.

*Nothing* comes up and slaps down
a doubloon on the granite counter
something he'd stolen from a treasure.
That should be enough he says
to claim all I ever owned
the full worth of my pretending.

My whole world implodes from body blows.
Stars collapse in the shock of a close call.
Knocks the full moon off its axis.
The last light I see divides
night from day, day from night.

Too slow to counter,
*Nothing* blocks my roundhouse.
Retaliates. Cutting through layers
of fat to expose raw nerve.
Down but not out

I rise on one knee, tracking the blur.
My armpits reek of loss.
My tires are flat.
Instincts carry dead weight
to a second wind.
Make him miss once, I think.
Then make him miss again.

## On the Bridge with Grey Owl

I dig into the archives and find another precedent.

Grey Owl, on his haunches, hunches over a sodden grief. Black robe
ripples twilight and his grey beard floats bodiless below parch-
ment-yellow eyes. In the I-beams above our heads he monitors
the slow progress of torches running along the dark river bank.

Those of us who made it to the bridge barely disentangle ourselves
from terrible witness, holding our intent, waving torches, carry-
ing signs. We will make a difference this time.

Grey Owl's literal eyes cross in a stew as he considers our appeal. The
sheer number of us bearing down, injured in the sudden rush to
the crossing, has quite visibly ruffled the old bird's feathers.

The bridge begins to tremble with our terrible weight. He flutters
loose jowls, shakes his head and hoots to a howl. *Overruled!*
*Overruled! Turn back NOW!*

On the bridge, we judge the distance from bank to bank. We've come
too far to turn back now.

*Denied. Denied!* he cries, gray matter like spittle righteously flung.

But the jury is still out.

Too close to the edge, we are bunched in a bottleneck inside steel
bones warped by last light. We shiver as the bridge yaws first to
the left then to the right. All perspective lost. The horizon drops
away. We come up rolling like drunks on a trampoline, leaning
into the wind, ankles braced for the fall.

# Floodstage

*"Residents living along the Grande Ronde River
should be ready to evacuate."*

Pellets of rain sting my face. This is no hoot in the hollow, I think,
watching the river rise.

Too long the winter, not letting go, a last howl clearing the street
of garbage cans, tin drums rolling away from drummers. Dark
clouds run high and fast, unmoored galleons grounded in the low
hills spilling bad luck that threatens muddy washes. Early walk-
ers, lifted onto toes, pushed home, wind at their back, gulping for
air as a gust hits them broadside.

I step back from the edge as the cutbank crumbles.

Later, back in my dark den, I recline in a leather lounge, sipping Ital-
ian roast and nibbling a toasted bagel.

During the night the river crested, high water inundated crops, over-
filled marshes, saturated sanctuaries of bird heaven. Mallards
and pintails swim circles around restless shallows, redwings on
cattails knock heads together.

Praise be, the flood water didn't reach us this year.

We're lucky.

# All My Walls Are Made of Glass

You learn humanity working with glass.
Cracks form under a clumsy hand.
It's what you do after the glass breaks
that makes the man. God bred my father
to be a brute sun, a harsh light that struck
the temple bell with a steel mallet.

I laid this weathered man
in an unmarked grave and threw dust over him.
I gave up the gun for the wheel,
pitched forward in the glare of first light,
'54 Ford pickup pointed down the straight and narrow.
My brothers in back bounced through a tunnel of dust
dragging bullfrogs with hooks in their mouths
laughing as they danced on the end of a fishing line.

Heckle and Jeckle, those two, crewcuts
like hardtack, never once aware
of the hooks in their own mouths until
blood ran down their chins.

*

The year of my birth was nailed on the wall
of a bone-dry topple-down shed quilted
with faded license plates—the once red paint
dun blasted by wind and rain.
My rearview fills up with screech owls
wings peeled by another long winter
and the glass breaks brother to brother

like father and son, touching
sharp edges with leather skin.

If I knew then what I know now
the rage would run out in a flash
evaporating on the dry creek bed.

\*

Going up Salt Creek, blasted and riding
on the fender of my brother's '55 Pontiac
I turned the spotlight on a blinded jack
blown dead in its tracks with a .30-30.
Only a clutch of hare and unlucky bloody foot
remained. Tormented light tracks us
even now to the dark side of a silver sage
to a lizard lounging on the creek bed
where fissures crack open.

## *To a Flicker In the Attic*

Have you given up, my angel?
I do not hear the thrashing of wings
in the dim-lived loft. From the thickest
thicket every revision descends

from somewhere above me
thrumming the shell of my gray habit
with urgent need. In the brittle warp
of black stars collapsing into my breast
still beating with wonder, I take
another wrong turn down
the wrong street
and end up here again.

I miss your tapping at my window
waking instead to false alarms.
How long did I spin sweet internal music
into the ravings of a deaf composer feeling vibrations
through spent, exhausted keys?

How many stones did I throw
before you found your wings?
You and I in the flash and flush
of flight carried from tree to tree to tree.
It's hard, these days, to hold an edge
to pull out of a tail spin
before you crash.

Have I seen the last of you?
I wonder.

# Caught In the Updraft

Entangled in thicket
you raise your voice and the wind slanders
your name. You lost the trail
a ways back, washed out in a flood, this way
the only one left open to the neutral zone.

Count from flash to thunderclap
the distance in seconds. Caretakers
watch vital signs
as a shiver intensifies into shell shock.
A weight holds you down.

Brush your wings.
From the first leap you might learn to fly
but first must lose the earth
flail and fall out of a cloud
upside down.

On the edge of a moving boundary
you can test your tolerance
for this *is* that.
Nothing more.

*Listen to me carefully*, she says,
*you must stay awake.*
*We need to remove the breathing tube.*

You were never meant
to stay here.

\*

The evergreens lean to whisper
in your ear. Lines that hold you together
in a taut web made of light
lift you into clouds like a crude kite
caught in the updraft.

# Spilling the Monsters

When he makes the bedsprings sing
from beaten brow a bright piccolo
quells the thick-as-jelly night

His sadness fills the room
as evening tilts and sadness leans his way
A child thumping his head

Thump, thump, thumping
Eyes and ears in a waking dream
dumping sees and saws
as he teetertotters up and down
at the edge of a soft sleep

fragments of mythology
from the mind's negative space
spilling from a swollen brain
restless with ragged voices

surfacing from a dull ocean roar
washed up spineless out of the sunless sea
not fully formed—jellyfish and squid
spilling from his head

Thump thumping in a soft sleep
riding the nightsea out in a drunken boat
swamped by writhing unwanted things

# III.

## Life Is a Beach

# *First Fish*

*It's been a long time since I've had blood on my hands*
—COMMERCIAL FISHERMAN

You can't ignore a leaky boat
says the man in the water.
Don't depend on someone
out of his element to pull you out.

Fish on a full moon, trust me
on this, the bigs won't rise to dead bait.
On a good day if the first fish
strikes you set the hook.

That's where it all begins—mad
run of albacore, jackpoled in the gills
and pulled kicking through a change
of worlds by a grinning fisherman.

*May the shadow of the moon,* the fisherman with blood
on his hands says, *fall on a world of peace.*

Tomorrow lies frozen on the bloody scale.
Bad news spreads quickly
on a leaky boat.

The fisherman catches
his breath and counts the wait.
A boat is only as good

as its crew. It's a good day
when the first fish strikes
and the hook is set.

More will come.

# *Waking Dream*

NEHALEM BAY

At the dock at dawn, the mist
rises from a drowned bay.
I unsling a crab ring with a whump
into the bottom of the boat and a great blue
breaks from the reeds, wingbeats
echoing over slack water.

We take the dinghy out and set a line.
I take the tiller;
you take the bait.

Dropping anchor in high tide, we wait out
the outgoing surge then ride high
in a slow drift, tying off fish heads
and lowering crab rings through refracted light.

I drift in this lucid dream: a rare event
I long for every day. A transient orca
rises out of my unconscious into the flow
cruising upriver in search of sea lions,
distinctive dorsal tracking like a periscope.

Under my arm I feel the sea change.
I pull against it. My mind in an ebb,
waterlogged in the channel, one half awake
the other half dreaming, full of blubber
scarred dorsal waving good-bye
as the dinghy pushes toward home.

\*

Dungeness piping hot from the crab pot
steam rising as we crack the shell
for sweet meat. Your knuckles stiff
from twisting wire, my shoulders sore
from holding course. Happy to live
this way, you and I, together in this waking dream
where freshwater and seawater meet.

# The Phantom Sailor Steers to the Stars

This storm will have us treading water.
We must be all in at this point
if we're to continue the plunder.

We could sever the moon from the tide
and ride the wave to where it breaks.
Adrift in a green galley in a whirling gale

rolled into a bay by a gray-white whale
up all night watching the sky
fill up with stars.

An open heart spills a bounty in the sand.
We must keep our eyes open for higher
ground, a place above the water line

to spread the charts and bend the light
and swing the sun through the seasons.
Aye, more have failed

who never tried, striking out
in a dinghy, head into the wind
where water meets sky.

The way was lost
before
the way was found.

# The Phantom Sailor Washes Up

AT SOUTH JETTY

With ship scuttled and lifeboat swamped
I drifted down feet-first, sleepwalking the seabed
like a crab, marched by the current
to landfall in a sputter of spume.
I could not feel my tongue laid cold
against chattering teeth, naked
white body glistening like jelly
in wet sand. The dull fact of drowning
was buried like a tick on a dog.

Nearly-mastered splices of life
gathered from the cutting room
floor were nailed to my coffin
played endlessly behind my eyelids.
Adrift in cold white light—the always
almost *nearly* of it fogged my breath—
waking on the soft edge of dissolution
in a bare-fisted bark
white wings of blinking canvas
lifting me over gelid edges
flayed and sewn windward
curing in cold white light.

Who would've known I'd make it this far
lying awake under the stars
a tale tattooed
on the white moon's chest.

# To the Man Carrying the Cross

ON OREGON HWY. 101

You hike bare-footed down the side of the road.
Ocean pounds the rocks below;
the rain forest breathes through fog.

I don't get to Paradise much these days
without driving past someone holy and homeless.
My sin is passing by.

How different are we, you and I?
We both wear beards and long hair
claim roots in the '60s.

\*

The world weighs on our shoulders.
We are bruised to the bone and have no strength
to carry the burden another step.

Who has not risen before dawn
trying to stay in their own lane, eyes on the road?
We both carry a cross with too many

miles to go. A sign
around our necks that reads:

BEGIN AGAIN!

## *Paean For the Molt*

Rockaway Beach, Oregon

We lie together silent under the hiss.
A dwindling number
unwilling to fly

more precious now than agate
more crab than bird or man
battered by the spent wave

The Harbor seal ducks under the waves
dancing to internal music.
We left our armor in the backwash

empty on the wet runway.
Stiff cold carapace. Bitter hollow
cog. Under a hungry eye

our soft bodies hung up in the rocks.

# IV.

## *A Feast Will Follow*

# The Christmas Tree Fire

In those days we lived in a log
home with dirt floors
in the forest where lamp and hearth
in the heart of winter was a rebirthed
evergreen dressed in tinsel
and topped with an angel.

The man in the picture, bent over
naked spruce, stacking dead
limbs for spring burning, is my father.
His head shaved like a monk.
Every year he saved the Christmas
tree and laid its withering bones
out back through the long nights
cover for the dickie birds.

Benign neglect turns a green limb
into tinder and lightning finds it waiting.
That's how the Christmas tree fire started.
Drought-dry spruce ignited in a flash.
I stood, mouth open, caught without a hose
as flames jumped to the wooden fence.

Last Christmas though, oh
you should have seen them, limbs lit
with light, softly embellished white chiffon
glazed with melt, tinsel sheen
shimmering still.

## *After the Ochoco Complex Fire*

Going south through charred spindles of ponderosa. Black roots splayed over fire-washed ground. They lean into apocalypse with the first hard rain.

My parents raised me to see the forest and not the trees whenever a jack pine fails, dead on its feet. Dry from drought a whole community goes up in a firebox struck by lightning. A new one can rise any minute in a hot wind that pops the serotinous seed.

We have not ended the genocide yet, our hunger to win pitches us forward like falling timber into mere board feet.

We have dropped the reins of Plato's chariot. The planet heats up and cooks the crab in the current and the jet stream whips up tortured spasms of dying worlds where another Atlantis sinks.

Our highways fill up with refugees.

The only invasion that matters from here is tumbleweed and ragwort, stubborn thistle taking a run at our most sacred spaces.

*September 2014*

# *Rainbird*

We spent our childhood in warm kitchens
around wood stoves, under the feet
of talkative women, our faces flushed
from heat billowing from the oven,
fresh bread and rhubarb pie piping hot
a generous slice sloughing into raw milk
marbled with sour sweet juice.

Uncle planted his victory garden,
*victory* claimed every spring from the hard scrabble
when rainbirds made the desert bloom.
Knee-high in sweet corn by mid-July, we pirouetted
to water jets arcing over serpentine vines
rows of luscious lettuce, pungent onion,
root vegetables thick as your arm.

At harvest time, we shucked the nested ears
for family reunion and thanked heaven
for another miracle coaxed
from the dust, miracles like hollyhocks
that dip down eye to eye standing in new light
cheeks warm with first blush.

In red rock canyons carved with shadow
where twisted limbs of limber pine
reach for the light and sand whispers over sandstone
what survives seems all the more human.

We could not prepare for how you left us, dear sister,
but behold what lives in memory:

the garden you brought forth,
the root system that took hold here in this desert,
the feast of love you laid on the table
for your children and your children's children.

\*

So when we gather to share our stories
we can hear your laughter still,
glimpse you walking under the *chit, chit, chit*
of the rainbird where rainbows melt

into mist.

*For my sister Kathy*

# Lunar Lullaby

Half-past five, Woody Woodpecker rides up our rearview. His grin chomping at the radiator screen of a shiny Kenworth. Tons of salvaged ponderosa pine bears down on the bumper of our poor Odyssey. I turn up the radio, step on the gas and we sail out over the edge of every curve just to stay in front of the mad push into Prineville.

That night, broken down on the side of the road at Ochoco Reservoir, brakes burned out, the siege ends with the dead fall behind us. The blackness of living networks destroyed by catastrophic fire. We sit at a picnic table listening to  barred owls reclaim the territory.

The ages of man ascend and descend in graceless order. We are embedded in a grand design we cannot see without these prosthetics. Our roots draw energy from the earth, our branches rise and spread, grown dense with words to pull down light from stars, intermingled with fibers of mycological myth anchored in a place called home.

Sitting here after the smoke clears, my belly pacified with a spoonful of peanut butter, I can feel the earth on my ribs. My skin vibrates in a full moon. I am a sound bowl rung by thunder. Waves of energy resonate with the drum of my heart. Star dust awakens a blood tide at the sound of your voice.

# Fossil Hunting in the Painted Hills

On a winding road in the Painted Hills
I steer a stony divide in the high desert
through worn-down treeless domes
descending on hair-pin turns.

At water's edge aroused with redwings
looking for a place to land
we drift into a slow glide in the shaded
shallows of the John Day

after miles of juniper and sage,
the cool current
soothing old wounds.
Some places, by design, geared

to take it slow, compose
with simple chemistry reunion
above and below of boom-busted
company towns and malignant reservations.

The river scores through time its own legacy
from the wide bend of the river
this rusted sepulcher beyond the scope
of my art collapses where

brown trout sleep
a tractor bleeds
into the flow where
the bank crumbles.

*For Sue, September 2014*

# *Friends Like Smoke*

Smoke caught me sleeping and moved in
during the night. I woke to find him
cooking eggs in bacon grease

and watching daytime t.v. He dropped in
from a wildfire and promised he wouldn't be
there for long. Weeks later he hasn't left

but squats in the recliner, feet up in slippers
wearing my robe. I see the humor in this
that's how he gets in and I get carried off in a golfcart

after another interception. I open Moose Drool
and scratch my balls, wondering about misfortune
while he's first in the shower every day.

My friends like Smoke, his jokes crack them up.
I see too much of my father in him
the memory installed in a gallery of soft crime

Too much of them I see in me, Smoke
and the man who made me
a mother defender baptized in a moment of rage.

There was no warning the day my dad
climbed into the attic with a gun.
But we should have seen it coming.

How do you prepare for a big blow?
They come without red flags and lift
the house off its foundation.

# Mother Worship

1.

We've come too far to turn back now.
The blue camas shimmers like a pluvial lake.
We dig in the mud for roots
Put bulbs into baskets and carry them
to the river to be pummeled with stone
and baked into hand cakes in hot rock ovens.

If everyone knew what we knew
it might spark the engine of creation.
Rewards for learning life skills
are a delicacy in fast food alley.
That flash of lightning unwitnessed among stars
reason enough to worship *here*
instead of *there.*

Auntie Em danced white sheets into a ball
as cumulus climbed dark and threatening
over a small farm in Kansas.
Batten down the hatches
lock the windows secure the doors
the witch is riding the wind again
on a windmill bike.

Where did the storm leave you?
It left me on the dry side of the Cascades
in a great round once a lake
with sandhill cranes wading in shallows
and mountain bluebirds filling up willows.

2.

Our mother never gets enough credit
for seeing us through the hard times. It takes
conscious effort to look back sometimes
to where we started in her arms
near the beat of her heart.

The land cannot stand up to these claims.
We fall backwards into an interior sea
slow dancing with moonlight on a cold plain
shagged with juniper.

*Not heaven* **on** *earth*, my mother says,
*heaven* **is** *earth.*

## *Mama Doesn't Cry*

mama doesn't cry when the rains
don't come
she remembers

when fire stole the dream
and built a house made of wood
on a dry plain with holes
for buttons and pockets to spare

mama made a home with a second husband
we called pa
who built calluses instead of castles
busted his knuckles keeping the engines running
and saw we never wanted for meat

first father was an angry god
who gambled on when to get in
 when to get out
his luck always about to turn

we are all his children

but she gave us life
we came back in the spring
with moods confused with colors

the numbers lie to us
how many will get over the pass
before they close it for winter?
we all do or none of us do

the road's always open on the leeward
the way made clear in moonlight
where blue camas rolls horizon to horizon

I walk in bunchgrass and wild rye on a sunny playa
see what I want to see

with the power to turn the forest into board feet
divert rivers into lakes, plant gardens in the dust
but leave ruts and gorges where Coyote
leaps over the moon

we are her children
we see what we want to see

A modest man who builds calluses
instead of castles comes home
for dinner every night

mama doesn't cry anymore
but she remembers

# A Feast Will Follow

## MORNING SONG

We are thankful for rest stops along the way, places we can sit in the shade sharing a cool rendezvous. On a small hill in the shadow of a mountain. We hike into the apple orchard at Badger Sett from moon to moon to drum and feast. Safe haven for animal spirits. Badger Sett is a second generation local story of Badger who stands back to the mountains, a stout dwarf tending the forge. He and Wolverine breed horses the color of dawn. Our den mother rides a dun horse to the sound of a drum. We share a lucid dream of our making, together, here in the orchard welcoming back the light.

We are loud in our celebration. Banging drums, blowing horns, shaking tambourines and rattles at the crack of dawn. We pull the light down to the earth into this apple grove, our jubilance carried into the wide valley below. Crow, Red-Tail and Mourning Dove check in to check out our ruckus in the hollow. We have gathered long enough now to call it a local tradition.

*

At the edge of night
and day we wait
for the sun.

She comes dressed in white
from the fertile dark
at the dawn of each new year.

We stand aside to make
a way for her. Build a fire
to help the light find a way.

She reaches us here
in a tangle of black branches,
in shadow under the hill

where we stamp cold feet
to the beat
of a buffalo drum.

When the white month moves
along the ridge, we leave behind
offerings:

cultured milk
white flour
sour cream.

*

Forty acres is a microcosm. We are embedded in the earth; the earth
is embedded in us. Drummers come to the sound of drums. They echo
and reply. Our common sphere resonates in a round dance with the
seasons. We mark how light rolls from ridge to ridge, down a ravine
in gravity's flow and dance with bells on. It has been a long winter
but the light has returned.

Pick up the beat. This is a celebration. There's elk stew in the pot and
white cakes with sour cream frosting after a song.

*

Sing this then in your own words,
it will mean the same:

O Mother of Light,
show us your face.
If thought be spark
that moves in waves
then mind makes light
as light makes day.

Where there be light
there be life;
where there be day
there be night.


for *Sagaalgan*, 2013

# Goldfinch In Sunflowers

What's invisible? Canary on canary.
If the art of camouflage confuses the eye
then goldfinch are magicians

keeping watch where heads of sunflower
unfurl soft coronas around a bounty of seed.
They glide down from the power line
into the garden you faithfully water every day.
By the time the white corn turns a silken ear
to the sweet nothings of golden birds
you send up a flare
from a dark interior where
you've fallen from the nest.

At last, the seed is ready.

Come get it!

## Crippled Bird

The living earth still breathes
lungs contract, the wind comes up
heart pumping currents
wave upon wave
cycles ending
cycles beginning
ready to ride
all the way back
the way we came

The crippled bird remains close to the nest;
he stretches his wings and fluffs his feathers
ready for flight, but barely lifts off the branch
before he stalls out
> what if he should go too far this time
> what if he cannot find his way back
> what if a sudden storm obliterates all landmarks
> or shadows deepen and absorb the sun?

The comfortable curve of the local
leads back to the nest, wounded wing
bending leeward in a world
made for only the right

Headstrong against a headwind
he finds a bold way out but loops back
again and again in an easy glide
a circular descent
round a place
called home

# The Echo Chamber

It's hard to stay alive in a land of the dead. I throw my voice against a wall, a solitary birdcall on the dark side of the moon.

The black door slides open.

I hear only echoes in the echo chamber. I knew this much when I left home for the hearing. They carved a great vault into the mountain to hold as many voices as possible. I practiced all my life to give my voice back in song before surrendering another octave. Even now I wait for word from my last audition.

*My time is coming*, I call down the Möbius strip.

Voices echo back, unrecognizable and reversed.

The dead cannot suppress their anger. The great vault fills up with it. Echoes without explanation. I hold my breath, waiting to join the chorus. With the right note in the right intervals, I might get a fair hearing.

Our keepers do not trust us to be alone with cacophony. Afraid we might make sense of twisted logic and untangle it to make some harmony.

Raw appeals can be fine-tuned and deepened with chords, anything to tone down the predilection for solos. Every voice can be heard yet no one voice identified.

Every voice an echo.

If I touch a keeper with something sublime, drawn from my personal repertoire, I might still make it new. They have heard so much already—voices echo back forever, soundwave overlapping soundwave—they are seldom surprised. They prefer nuance to loudness. Their tastes are very refined.

The keeper took my voice and promised to lock it into a wooden box until it has been properly reversed and released. Still, if a good word comes back, I might not even recognize it.

It's hard to stay alive in a land of the dead. I throw my voice against a wall, a solitary birdcall on the dark side of the moon.

# End-of-the-World Cinema

I stand at land's end at twilight. A salvaged ship floats up, its deck
lit up like a carnival, rotating slowly in the fog. A bright beam like
that of a moving picture projects through light years, pierces a field
of stars, and projects titles I cannot read as my body swoons to a
rudderless boat.

From light years of flickering dreams, the pilot lets down a ladder.
I climb—dizzy and barely able to hang on—as the disk turns on its
own axis.

We are old movies narrowed down to a particle stream, our
movements jerky and cosmic as our screen flickers to life. Take a
seat. See yourself.

Moving pictures projected back from a time light years later reduced
from a wave to a particle. Immersed in your own story unpacked
by machines.

What happens in the crossing doesn't happen just to you. We all
come to catch small episodes that unspool and spool again.

Take a seat. Your story is not yet over. And it never ends when
you think.

*She was the single artificer of the world*
*In which she sang. And when she sang, the sea*
*Whatever self it had, became the self*
*That was her song...*
          —WALLACE STEVENS

# A View From the Summit

From where I stand looking back
on the dual-tracked trail that winds
up the steep canyon like narrow gauge
the exercise makes sense to me now.
I have always followed tracks
scissored through naked larch undressed by wind
from the comfortable rut of my practice.

Cocooned in silence, breaking new trail
I climb the mountain, exposed and unsure,
precious heat lost with every breath.
Alone at the summit, my nerves numb
from ground chill rising through flesh
I stand alone, bent to the scent of your blood
in black tracks on a field of white fire.

I feel you watching from a place unseen
made possible by where I've been,
beyond the unbroken line in the bright snow.
I take back with me to a warm den
this possibility of a perfect glide
on a well-defined track
each stride and stroke

unfaltering.

# Acknowledgments

Many people deserve thanks for contributions to this book. The critical feedback and support of my writing group—James Benton, Amelia Diaz Ettinger, Nancy Knowles, Thomas Madden and George Venn. Their guiding light and clear vision gave me confidence to cross-pollinate and endowed me with the grace to assemble poems into a book. I owe special thanks to Dave Mehler, editor of *Triggerfish,* for reading a much earlier version of this manuscript and offering invaluable feedback. James Ambrosek and John Morrison also provided critical thoughts at critical stages. I could not have gotten to this far without them.

I owe a debt of gratitude to Greg Johnson and Kristin Summers of Redbat Books for their belief in me and for the flexibility to follow my mercurial impulse to revise up to the last minute. The book came together after two years of revising and adding and subtracting, but I declare this FINAL.

"Spilling the Monsters" is a revision of the poem of the same title published in an earlier collection, *Giving It Away* (2009). Grateful acknowledgment is given to the following journals in which poems have appeared in some earlier version.

*Basalt:* "Paean for the Molt"
*Cirque:* "View from the Summit"
*Gargoyle* (40th Anniversary Issue): "Caught in the Updraft,"
    "Some Nights My Nothing Rises"
*Mithila Review* (India): "The Echo Chamber"
*Phantom Drift 11*: "The Phantom Sailor Washes Up,"
    "End-of-the-World Cinema"
*Sheila-Na-Gig* online: "After the Ochoco Complex Fire"
*The Poeming Pigeon*: "Fossil Hunting in the Painted Hills"
*Triggerfish:* "Path of Least Resistance," "Starlings in Winter"
*Weber: The Contemporary West:* "To the Squirrel Who Ate the Suet,"
    "Small Matters Mean the World," "In Potentia: A Revision"
*Willawaw Journal,* "Mother Worship"

## About the Author

David Memmott has been living and writing in the Pacific Northwest most of his life. His work explores views of the American West, personal and mythic, rural and progressive. His long poem, "Where the Yellow Brick Road Turns West," from the collection *Lost Transmissions*, was a finalist for the Spur Award. Poems have appeared recently in *basalt, Cirque, Gargoyle, Sheila-Na-Gig, The Poeming Pigeon, Triggerfish: A Critical Review, Weber: The Contemporary West* and *Willawaw Journal.* He founded *Phantom Drift: A Journal of New Fabulism* and Wordcraft of Oregon. His digital art and other samples of his writings can be accessed through his website at: davidmemmott.com

www.ingramcontent.com/pod-product-compliance
Lightning Source LLC
Chambersburg PA
CBHW031146090426
42738CB00008B/1237